Missa 'Cantate'

Bob Chilcott

for SATB choir and optional piano

Vocal score

MUSIC DEPARTMENT

OXFORD
UNIVERSITY PRESS

OXFORD
UNIVERSITY PRESS

Great Clarendon Street, Oxford OX2 6DP, England
198 Madison Avenue, New York, NY 10016, USA

Oxford University Press is a department of the University of Oxford.
It furthers the University's aim of excellence in research, scholarship,
and education by publishing worldwide in

Oxford New York
Auckland Cape Town Hong Kong Karachi
Kuala Lumpur Madrid Melbourne Mexico City Nairobi
New Delhi Shanghai Taipei Toronto

With offices in

Argentina Austria Brazil Chile Czech Republic France Greece
Guatemala Hungary Italy Japan Poland Portugal Singapore
South Korea Switzerland Thailand Turkey Ukraine Vietnam

Oxford is a registered trade mark of Oxford University Press
in the UK and in certain other countries

ISBN 978-0-19-335638-2

Music origination by
Enigma Music Production Services, Amersham, Bucks.
Printed in Great Britain on acid-free paper by
Halstan & Co. Ltd., Amersham, Bucks.

Contents

Composer's note

This is the third setting I have written of the shortened Mass. Having sung so many great Mass settings myself, I have always been aware of the drama, colour, feeling, and sense of devotion that reside in the text.

Missa 'Cantate' was written as a response to a request from Michael Kibblewhite, conductor of the Cantate Youth Choir, for a piece that would challenge a young choir of both female and male voices, where the male voice part is fundamentally unison. The piece is basically a cappella, but if preferable the piano can be added in the Kyrie, Gloria, and Benedictus. It is also effective to include some percussion accompaniment in the Gloria.

Duration: c.10 minutes

Commissioned by Cantate Youth Choir and Pax Travel
for the enjoyment of Cantate's young singers directed by
Michael Kibblewhite

Missa 'Cantate'

BOB CHILCOTT

1. *Kyrie*

Chri - ste, Chri - ste, e - le - i - son, Chri - ste, Chri - ste e - le - i - son, Chri -

Chri - ste, Chri - ste, e - le - i - son, Chri - ste, Chri - ste e - le - i - son, Chri -

- ste, Chri - ste, e - le - i - son, Chri - ste, Chri - ste e - le - i - son,

- ste, Chri - ste e - le - i - son, e - le - i - son.

- ste, Chri - ste e - le - i - son, e - le - i - son.

Chri - ste, Chri - ste e - le - i - son, e - le - i - son.

2. Gloria

Rex coe - le - stis, De - us Pa - ter om - ni - po - tens, Do - mi - ne___ Fi - li

u - ni - ge - ni - te, Je - su Chri - ste,___ Je - su Chri - ste.

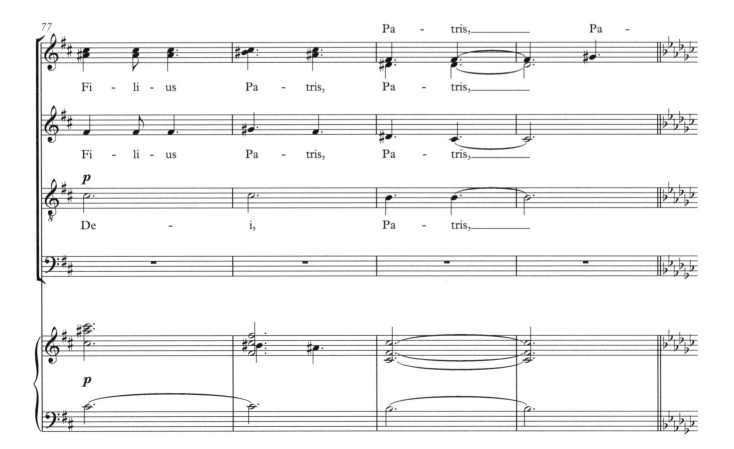

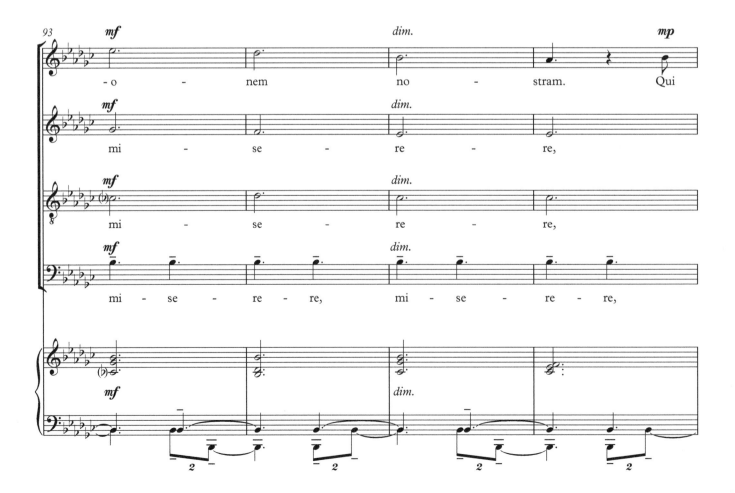

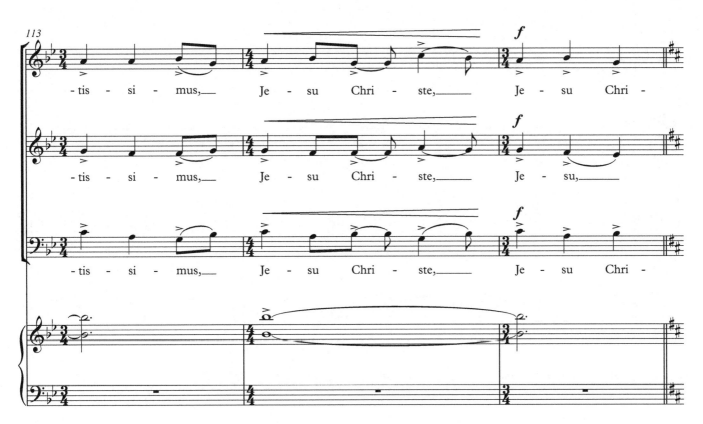

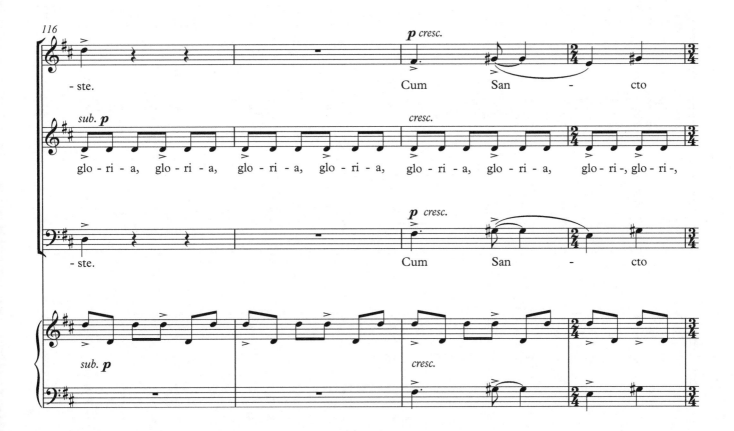

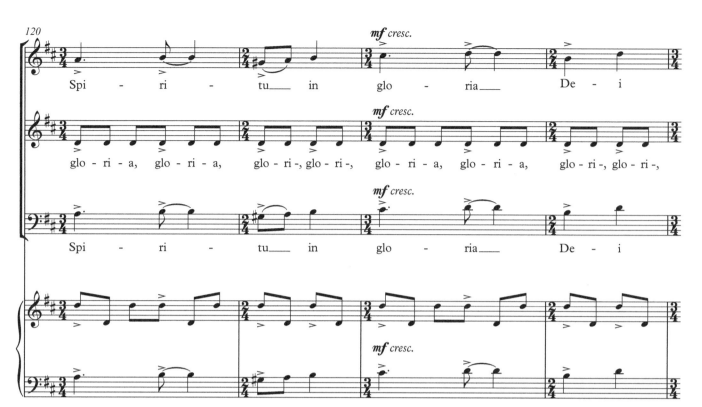

gloria Dei Patris, in gloria Dei Patris, Amen.

3. *Sanctus*

With simplicity and warmth ♩ = c.56

San - ctus, san - ctus Do - mi - nus De - us Sa - ba - oth,

for rehearsal only

San - ctus,____ san - ctus Do - mi - nus De - us Sa - ba - oth.____

San - ctus,____ san - ctus Do - mi - nus De - us Sa - ba - oth.____

San - ctus,____ san - ctus Do - mi - nus De - us Sa - ba - oth,____

San - ctus,____ san - ctus Do - mi - nus De - us Sa - ba - oth,____

San - ctus,____ san - ctus Do - mi - nus De - us Sa - ba - oth,____

Sanctus, sanctus Dominus Deus Sabaoth. Ple-

Sanctus, sanctus Dominus Deus Sabaoth. Ple-

Sanctus, sanctus Dominus Deus Sabaoth. Ple-

-ni sunt coe-li et ter-ra glo-ri-a, glo-ri-a tu-a. Ho-

-ni sunt coe-li et ter-ra glo-ri-a, glo-ri-a tu-a. Ho-

-ni sunt coe-li et ter-ra glo-ri-a, glo-ri-a tu-a. Ho-

4. *Benedictus*

be - ne - dic - tus, be - ne - dic - tus, be - ne - dic - tus, be - ne - dic - tus.

be - ne - dic - tus, be - ne - dic - tus, be - ne - dic - tus, be - ne - dic - tus.

no - mi - ne Do - mi - ni.

in no - mi - ne Do - mi - ni.

Be - ne - dic - tus, be - ne-dic - tus, be - ne-dic - tus qui ve - nit,

Be - ne - dic - tus qui ve - nit

Be - ne - dic - tus qui ve - nit, be - ne -

5. *Agnus Dei*

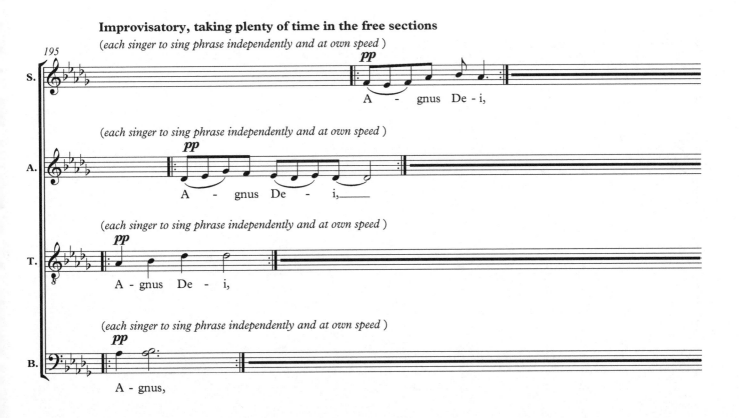

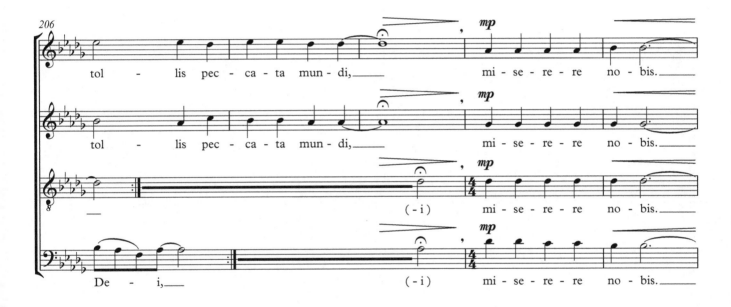

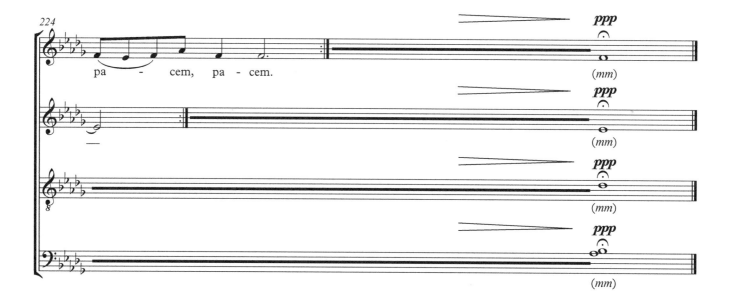